SEASHELLS, SANIBEL ISLAND

(Pages 2-3) GREAT EGRETS AND WHITE IBISES, SOUTH
FLORIDA. The dictates of fashion in the late 19th and early 20th
centuries led to the slaughter of such birds for their plumage.
While protective legislation has saved some species from extinction, safeguarding their wetland habitat remains a challenge.

(Pages 4-5) TAMPA. Constructed in the 1970s and early 1980s,
office buildings rise above downtown Tampa. During the Spanish-
American War, Theodore Roosevelt and his Rough Riders were
among the thousands who embarked for Cuba from this port city.

(Pages 6-7) FORT LAUDERDALE. A six-mile beach stretches
before the city built on the site of a frontier fortress commanded
by Major William Lauderdale in the late 1830s.

REFLECTED SABAL PALMS, ALACHUA COUNTY

Published by Thomasson-Grant, Inc., Frank L. Thomasson III and John F. Grant, Directors
Designed by Carolyn F. Weary and Megan R. Youngquist
Edited by Elizabeth L. T. Brown and Carolyn M. Clark
Copyright © 1988 by Thomasson-Grant, Inc. All rights reserved.
Photographs copyright © 1988 by photographers as attributed on page 95.
Marjorie Kinnan Rawlings, excerpted from *Cross Creek*.
Copyright 1942 Marjorie Kinnan Rawlings;
copyright renewed © 1970 Norton Baskin.
Reprinted with the permission of Charles Scribner's Sons.
This book, or any portions thereof, may not be reproduced in any form
without written permission of the publisher, Thomasson-Grant, Inc.
Library of Congress Catalog Card Number: 87-50690
ISBN 0-934738-32-7
Printed and bound in Japan by Dai Nippon Printing Co., Ltd.
95 94 93 92 91 90 89 88   4 3 2 1
Any inquiries should be directed to the publisher, Thomasson-Grant, Inc.,
One Morton Drive, Suite 500, Charlottesville, VA 22901,
telephone (804) 977-1780.

THOMASSON-GRANT

FLORIDA
·REDISCOVERED·

Compiled by C. Douglas Elliott and Jeffrey B. Trammell

CAPITOL, TALLAHASSEE

As they have since the 19th century, thousands of visitors come to Florida each year. Seeking a week's refuge from ice and rain, many do not have time to venture beyond the most popular beaches and tourist attractions to see the state which, although just as warm and appealing, is also a place of unexpected, sometimes bizarre beauty, and of real-world complexity. Before we began this book, the best we felt we could do when we met people who had never had an opportunity to visit the Florida we love was to give them a copy of something by Marjorie Kinnan Rawlings, the writer who made a corner of Alachua County her own through the pages of such works as "Gal Young 'Un," the autobiographical *Cross Creek,* and the classic novel of a boy's passage into manhood, *The Yearling.* In 1928 at the age of 32, Rawlings moved from Rochester, New York, to Cross Creek and found there a Florida beyond any travel agent's or realtor's promise, a place where, as she wrote:

> Enchantment lies in different things for each of us. For me, it is in this: to step out of the bright sunlight into the shade of orange trees; to walk under the arched canopy of their jadelike leaves; to see the long aisles of lichened trunks stretch ahead in a geometric rhythm; to feel the mystery of a seclusion that yet has shafts of light striking through it. This is the essence of an ancient and secret magic....Here is home. An old thread, long tangled, comes straight again.

The enchantment lies also in thunderclouds building above the Kissimmee Prairie, sunlight glinting from the newly washed windows of a skyscraper in downtown Tampa, and springs of such mysterious splendor that it is easy to believe, as is reputed, that Samuel Taylor Coleridge was reading a description of them before he dreamed the visionary poem fragment "Kubla Khan" and wrote of Xanadu. Everyone familiar with Florida could add others, for there is no single way to capture the essence of so varied a state, especially when that essence has inspired such insistent romanticism.

Florida has always lent itself to overstatement. In 1563, Jean Ribaut wrote in *The Whole and True Discoverye of Terra Florida:*

> It is a place wonderfull fertill, and of strong scituation, the ground fat so that it is lekely that it would bring fourthe wheate and all other corn twise a yeare...yt is a country full of havens, rivers and islandes of suche frute- fullnes as cannot with tonge be expressed...altrough yt be one of the goodly- est, best and frutfullest cuntres that ever was sene, and where nothing lacketh.

Sometimes the beauty Rawlings described nearly 400 years later seems almost excessive, like the scent of orange blossoms so strong it can be detected miles out at sea. Florida overwhelms. At times the same sun which burns the skin of unwary visitors can also blind photographers to the landscape's more subtle moods.

In looking at thousands of photographs to find those we felt best conveyed our vision of the state, we realized how stereotypes tend to obscure a more complicated and intriguing Florida. Although its human history dates back some 12,000 years, long before the 1565 founding of St. Augustine, many Floridians themselves do not realize, for example, that their state was a loyal British colony during the American Revolution and a member of the Confederacy during the Civil War, or that the seeds of the Spanish-American War were nurtured in the cigar factories of Tampa.

Since 1513, the official flags of Spain, France, Great Britain, the Confederacy, and the United States, as well as a number of unofficial ones, have flown over Florida. There are times when we, like residents of any place with a distinct tourist appeal, have felt most in sympathy with the banner presented to incoming Governor William D. Moseley in 1845 when Florida was admitted to the Union; its motto declared, "Let us alone." Nevertheless tourism is a colorful and important part of the state's traditions.

George M. Barbour, in his 1883 publication *Florida for Tourists, Invalids, and Settlers,* declared:

> a settler in Florida—whether he comes as a capitalist, as a farmer, or as a laborer—can live with more ease and personal comfort, can live more cheaply, can enjoy more genuine luxuries, can obtain a greater income from a smaller investment and by less labor, and can sooner secure a competency, than in any other accessible portion of North America.

Written at a time when steamboats churned along many of Florida's rivers, already bringing countless travelers to resorts like Silver Springs, Barbour's words, while perhaps less poetic than those of Ribaut and Rawlings, proved equally attractive. Before the turn of the 20th century, two farsighted developers, Henry Flagler and

CINDERELLA CASTLE, WALT DISNEY WORLD

Henry Plant, began extending their railroad lines down the peninsula's east and west coasts and building hotels to accommodate their passengers. Along the rails, towns became cities. By the 1920s, Tin Can Tourists, named for the way they stored food in the back seats of their cars, traveled the state's roads. Some of the nation's wealthiest families wintered in Boca Raton, Miami, and Palm Beach, enjoying the exuberant excesses captured by the Marx Brothers' film *The Cocoanuts.*

Good times were clearly to be had in Florida; its promise of pleasure and profit became part of the American consciousness. Although in 1926 hurricane winds shattered buildings along the lower east coast and paper millionaires joined the bread lines, neither natural nor economic disaster could dim the state's luster. Between 1920 and 1940, Florida's population doubled; it has been climbing steadily since.

Some 6,000 new residents arrive weekly, and whether or not they find the kind of life George M. Barbour touted, they will quickly discover a Florida beyond the surf and souvenir stands. Cowboys are as much a part of the state as college students at Fort Lauderdale. Collard greens, spiced shrimp, and *arroz con pollo* complement citrus flavors. Alligators lumber across golf course greens.

Too frequently the impressions that Florida's visitors take home with them are like pink plastic flamingos—fun, but artificial. While young women dressed in glittering fish tails perform for crowds at Weeki Wachee, other Florida waters harbor manatees, the rare marine mammals that inspired lonely sailors to weave the mermaid legend. More Americans may recognize the 198-foot spire of Walt Disney World's Cinderella Castle, but the 32-foot walls of St. Augustine's Castillo de San Marcos repeatedly protected the citizens of this Spanish outpost from attack in the 1700s; their failure would have altered the shape of Florida's, and perhaps the nation's, history.

Today many of the state's eight million public acres are set aside for the protection of wildlife and the fragile ecosystems that nourish it. Unfortunately, the ability to enjoy beauty without coveting it is a recent development, one which came too late to save Florida's wild flamingos. The wading birds John James Audubon admired when he visited Key West in the

CASTILLO DE SAN MARCOS, ST. AUGUSTINE

1830s were slaughtered to extinction for their magnificent feathers. Coral flocks now wandering the grounds of Hialeah Park are captive, imported from Cuba in the late 1930s. The stilt-legged bird that once touched Florida's skies with rose has become a cliché.

In every way, the facts about Florida are more complex and interesting than the fictions. Ponce de León, for example, was a tough-minded and practical man who named Florida for the church season during which he made his 1521 landing, and not for its blossoms. He came in search of gold and power, not a Fountain of Youth. He left the area of what is now Charlotte Harbor with a fatal arrow wound.

Sands redolent of suntan oil were once stained with blood; during the turbulent years of the Seminole Wars, William Techumseh Sherman remarked, "This country is not worth a damn." Florida's history, like that of most places, belies its image; its people have fought, loved, suffered, exulted, and lived their lives with dignity of a sort rarely mentioned in slick advertisements or newspaper headlines.

Describing her emotions on coming to Florida, Rawlings wrote in *Cross Creek* that "the joining of person to place, as of person to person, is a commitment to shared sorrow, even as to shared joy." Those of us who love Florida as she did recognize a similar commitment. Ours is one of the fastest-growing states in the nation, and while the problems growth brings are undeniably challenging, Florida's future is bright.

Increasingly, Floridians and indeed all Americans are learning to treasure the state's historic and natural heritage. They are working to preserve what is best about Florida so that it will continue to reward those who linger for a closer look with reason to believe, like Jean Ribaut, that the place they have found is "one of the goodlyest, best and frutfullest cuntres that ever was sene."

C. Douglas Elliott
Jeffrey B. Trammell

(Left) CANOPIED ROAD, LEON COUNTY. Spanish moss is an air plant, not a parasite; the branches it drapes merely provide support for the rootless moss which absorbs moisture through its leaves. Until the late 1950s, Spanish moss was used commercially to fill seat cushions, chairs, and mattresses.

THE GROVE, TALLAHASSEE. Informed by convention delegates of Florida's secession from the Union on January 10, 1861, future governor Richard Keith Call of The Grove said, "You have opened the gates of hell." Although few battles were waged on Florida's soil, over 15,000 Floridians fought in the Civil War.

PECAN GROVE, SUWANNEE COUNTY. Pecans, peanuts, soybeans, hay, and tobacco are among the crops grown in the rural areas of north Florida. The commercial use of the region's pine forests for such products as plywood, pulpwood, paper, and paperboard boxes is also important to the state's economy.

19TH-CENTURY HOUSE, TALLAHASSEE. Founded in 1824 to serve as the seat of state government, Tallahassee was the only Confederate capital east of the Mississippi never occupied by Union troops. A city whose major business is government, it is still graced with Spanish moss and houses like this one built in 1879.

OYSTER BOATS, ST. GEORGE ISLAND. Oysters harvested from more than 10,000 acres of beds are a major source of income in the Apalachicola area.

BROWN PELICAN, NORTH FLORIDA. Bulky birds with a six-foot wingspread, brown pelicans often fly close to the water in single file, then plunge abruptly beneath the surface to scoop up fish in their pouches. They are one of approximately 325 bird species native to the state.

GHOST CRAB, NORTH FLORIDA. Among the scavengers that scuttle across the sands of Florida's Gulf Coast is this small, burrowing crustacean.

SEA OATS, ST. GEORGE ISLAND. The long tap roots of sea oats help stabilize shifting dunes and fight beach erosion.

BIRD DOGS, NORTH FLORIDA. The quail these dogs hunt are found throughout the state, along with squirrels, rabbits, opossums, foxes, and raccoons. Larger game includes white-tailed deer, bears, and wild hogs, descendants of domestic pigs which escaped from early settlements.

TOBACCO BARN, NEAR GRETNA. Florida's aboriginal Indians smoked tobacco long before Europeans arrived. By the time of the Civil War, the plant had become an important source of revenue.

SUWANNEE RIVER. The river made famous by a Pennsylvanian composer's quest for a mellifluous southern place name flows from Georgia's Okefenokee Swamp into the Gulf of Mexico. Stephen Foster's "Old Folks at Home" is Florida's state song.

(Right) SABAL PALMS, FAKAHATCHEE STRAND. A hardy and majestic tree, the sabal palm grows throughout Florida. It was designated the state tree in 1953 and in 1970 replaced the endangered coconut palm on the state seal.

LAKE, NEAR HAWTHORNE. More than 7,700 lakes dot Florida's landscape, including Okeechobee, the nation's second largest freshwater lake within the borders of a single state.

CYPRESS TREES, WAKULLA SPRINGS. Unlike most other conifers, cypress trees are deciduous. Some naturalists believe that the conical "knees" which project up through the water around them help stabilize cypresses rooted in loose organic debris; others speculate that they help the trees breathe.

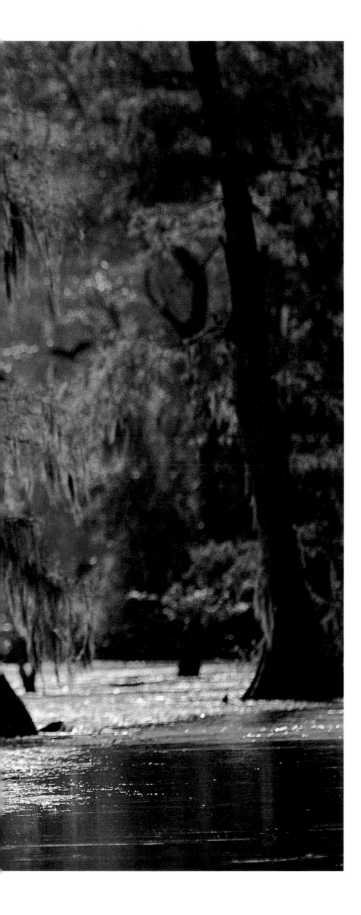

TUGBOAT, NORTH FLORIDA. Most of Florida's major rivers are of the blackwater type, their characteristic dark color leached from the tannic acid of pine forests and swamps.

SHRIMP BOATS, FERNANDINA BEACH. When Amelia Island's fishermen replaced their rowboats and hand seines with motor-powered trawlers in the early part of the 20th century, their livelihood developed into today's high-volume shrimp industry.

ST. JOHNS RIVER, JACKSONVILLE. A city-county consolidation in 1968 made what was once a cattle crossing the nation's largest city in land area. Straddling the St. Johns River, Jacksonville, founded in 1822, now covers 841 square miles.

HORSE FARM, NEAR OCALA. The 1956 Kentucky Derby victory of a horse named Needles first brought Florida's potential as a Thoroughbred-breeding state to national attention. Since then, three other Derby winners have been bred in Florida; only Kentucky and California raise more Thoroughbreds.

THUNDERSTORM, CENTRAL FLORIDA. An annual rainfall of 53 inches makes Florida one of the nation's wettest states. Much of this precipitation seeps underground, replenishing Florida's limestone aquifers.

ORANGES, LAKE COUNTY. Florida's first oranges arrived on Spanish ships before 1567; wild citrus groves were prevalent in many parts of the peninsula by the mid-1700s. Today the state produces over 70 percent of the nation's oranges, grapefruit, lemons, limes, tangerines, and tangelos.

(Right) ORANGE GROVE, LAKE COUNTY. Although Florida's earliest commercial groves were planted in the late 1800s, the citrus industry's most dramatic growth came after the development of frozen juice concentrate in the 1940s.

(*Left*) RAINBOW SPRINGS, MARION COUNTY. Flori[d]
springs, like many of its lakes, are fed by reservoirs o[f]
trapped in the porous limestone cap underlying most [of the]
peninsula. No other state has more first-magnitude sprin[gs than]
Florida; 27 springs produce a total average flow of [more than]
billion gallons each day.

WEST INDIAN MANATEES, CRYSTAL RIVER. Con[suming]
up to 100 pounds of aquatic plants each day, the manate[e feeds]
and winters in the warm coastal waters of Florida's rivers[. Speed-]
ing motor boats pose the most serious threat to this [rare,]
endangered marine mammal.

(*Pages 40-41*) SALT MARSH, PASCO COUNTY. Ferti[le ham-]
mocks, "islands" of broad-leaved trees surrounded by [low]
shrubs and plants, like this one in a marsh near Aripe[ka, are]
common throughout Florida's swamps, pinelands, and [marshes.]

(Left) SKYSCRAPER WITH REFLECTION OF OLD CITY HALL, TAMPA. In the late 1800s, developer Henry Plant's South Florida Railroad, Vincente Martinez Ybor's cigar factory, and nearby phosphate fields brought new prosperity to Tampa, now Florida's third most populous city.

SUNSHINE SKYWAY BRIDGE, TAMPA BAY. Before 1954, a ferry shuttled across the mouth of Tampa Bay between St. Petersburg and Palmetto.

DON CESAR HOTEL, ST. PETERSBURG BEACH.
F. Scott and Zelda Fitzgerald are said to have stayed
at this 277-room hotel built in the late 1920s. During
World War II, the Don Cesar was used as a conva-
lescent center for airmen.

RINGLING MUSEUM OF ART, SARASOTA. Part of a fortune earned by "The Greatest Show on Earth" went to house the art collection of circus magnate John Ringling in the 1920s. The museum, modeled after a 15th-century Florentine villa, includes paintings by Peter Paul Rubens.

WINTER HOME OF THOMAS ALVA EDISON, FORT MYERS. Edison built his winter residence in 1886. The creator of the light bulb perfected numerous other inventions at this house, which boasts one of Florida's first modern swimming pools.

BARRIER ISLANDS, PINE ISLAND SOUND. Florida has more
islands than any other state except Alaska. At least 4,510 of
these are ten acres or larger.

(Left) CAYO COSTA, PINE ISLAND SOUND. Most of this island's 2,200 acres belong to the state, set aside as a refuge for birds and for people who enjoy seclusion and primitive camping.

RAILROAD VINE MORNING GLORIES, CAYO COSTA. Hardy plants well adapted to survival on shifting sands, railroad vine morning glories cling to the beach of this sparsely inhabited barrier island which once served as a U.S. Navy quarantine.

JETTY, PALM BEACH. The palms that gave one of the nation's most exclusive communities its name are said to have been planted by pioneer families from coconuts washed ashore following the wreck of a Spanish ship in 1878.

POLO PLAYERS, PALM BEACH. From December to April, polo matches attracting top players from around the world, including the Prince of Wales, are held on over 20 fields in the Palm Beach area.

(Right) ESTATE, PALM BEACH. Real estate prices around Lake Worth skyrocketed when Henry Flagler announced his intention to build a hotel in Palm Beach in the early 1890s. By the 1920s, the community had gained a reputation for the flamboyance of its Spanish-influenced buildings and their affluent occupants.

(*Left*) BARRED OWLS, CORKSCREW SWAMP SANCTUARY. One of only two brown-eyed owl species in the eastern United States, the barred owl nests in the cavities of trees like this cypress and feeds on small birds, rodents, frogs, lizards, crayfish, and insects.

BROMELIAD, SOUTH FLORIDA. Related to the pineapple, these rootless epiphytes, nonparasitic plants which grow on other plants, catch and store water in the bases of their leaves. This enables them to survive winter droughts and thrive in a semi-tropical climate.

ROSEATE SPOONBILLS AND SNOWY EGRETS, SOUTH
FLORIDA. The spatulate beak which the roseate spoonbill
swings from side to side while feeding is unique among wading
birds in the United States. Immature spoonbills are faint pink;
their color intensifies with age.

(Right) ALLIGATORS, SOUTH FLORIDA. An endangered
species as recently as the 1960s, alligators are now so common
in Florida that they occasionally wander up canals into suburban
swimming pools. Hatchlings are roughly eight inches long;
mature males often measure up to 13 feet.

(Left) WETLANDS, CORKSCREW SWAMP SANCTUARY. The National Audubon Society, founded in response to the whole-sale slaughter of birds at the turn of the 20th century, owns and operates this 11,000-acre wilderness area. The sanctuary is noted for its large stand of virgin bald cypresses, some of which are over 500 years old.

ANHINGA, SOUTH FLORIDA. Its snake-like neck and fan-shaped tail give this bird two other names: snake bird and water turkey. The anhinga spears fish with its sharp bill, then flips them into the air to catch and swallow them headfirst. Like several other bird species in Florida, it will not nest during periods of drought.

BRAFORD CATTLE, KISSIMMEE PRAIRIE. In 1521, Ponce de León brought the first cattle—six Andalusian heifers and a bull—to Florida's shores. The introduction of Brahman cattle, the only breed with sweat glands, led to the crossbreeding of animals able to gain weight despite the heat.

(Right) GRASSHOPPER AND COWBOY, SOUTH FLORIDA. During the Civil War, cattle drives of up to 40 days' duration supplied Confederate troops with beef. Cattle ranged freely over much of the state as recently as 1949.

TRUCK FARM, DADE COUNTY. Enriched by marl and the centuries-old muck of decayed saw grass, the soil of reclaimed wetlands around Lake Okeechobee supplies the nation with such vegetables as lettuce, radishes, snap beans, celery, cabbage, and cucumbers.

HARVESTED SUGARCANE, DADE COUNTY. Syrup boiled from crushed cane sweetened the meals of early Floridians. After trade between the United States and Cuba ceased in 1961, the production of sugarcane assumed new importance in the economy of Florida, now the nation's largest sugarcane grower.

(Left) SAILBOATS, MIAMI. A mild climate, scores of sheltered harbors, and over 8,426 miles of tidal shoreline make Florida excellent for sailing and other types of boating. More than 170 drawbridges accommodate maritime traffic.

FISHING PIER, MIAMI. Some 1,200 species of fish, among them black mullet, king mackerel, red snapper, tarpon, sailfish, and pompano, live in Florida's salt waters.

THE CARLYLE, MIAMI BEACH. Rapid development during
Miami Beach's early years led to unusual architectural uniformity.
Structures built in the 1920s drew inspiration from Mediterranean
models; those built in the 1930s were of the *moderne* style, more
popularly known as art deco.

ART DECO BUILDING, MIAMI BEACH. In 1979, some 800 structures in the Miami Beach Architectural District, many of which reflect the fluid forms, geometric shapes, and pastel shades popular during the 1930s, were added to the National Register of Historic Places.

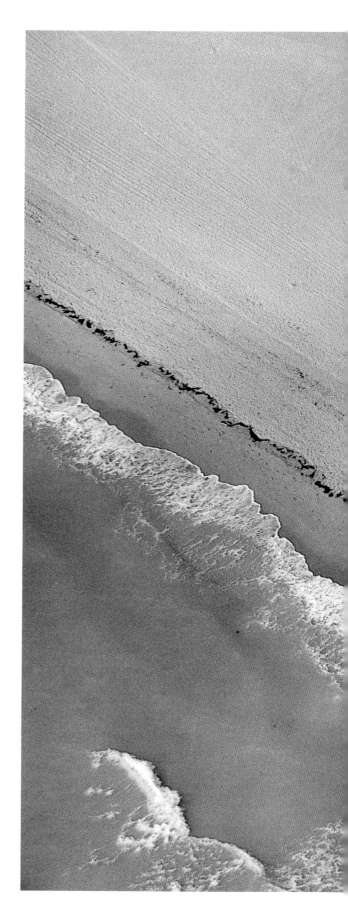

HOT DOG VENDOR, MIAMI BEACH. Over 30 million people visit Florida each year, making tourism one of the state's major industries.

MIAMI BEACH. Approximately 780 miles of Florida's coastline, the United States' second longest, are sand beaches. Along the southeast coast, the average temperature in January is around 70°.

INTRACOASTAL WATERWAY, MIAMI BEACH. A tourist from Indianapolis, Carl Fisher, was among those instrumental in the development of what was little more than a sandbar before 1915. Fisher financed the resort's causeway, built its first hotels, and dredged Biscayne Bay to create Miami Beach.

VILLA VIZCAYA, BISCAYNE BAY. Industrialist James Deering was one of the many wealthy people attracted to Miami in the early 1900s. His palatial Italianate villa, built in 1916, now houses the Vizcaya Museum.

CAPE FLORIDA LIGHTHOUSE, KEY BISCAYNE. Early European maps delineating the Florida peninsula suggest that John and Sebastian Cabot may have sailed as far south as Cape Florida in the 1490s. The Cape Florida Lighthouse, once known as the Spanish Light, was built in 1825.

WETLANDS, BIG CYPRESS NATIONAL PRESERVE. Established in 1974 to serve as an ecological buffer for the adjacent Everglades National Park, this national preserve covers less than half of the Big Cypress Swamp.

(Right) MICCOSUKEE INDIAN, SOUTH FLORIDA. The Miccosukees trace their ancestry to Indians who eluded the U.S. Army following the Second Seminole War in the mid-1800s.

SAW GRASS AND MANGROVES, EVERGLADES. Once saw grass, named for its sharp, serrated leaves, covered some three million acres in the Everglades, where it remains the dominant vegetation. Mangroves provide a rich habitat for animal life above and below the salt water in which they grow.

(Right) LITTLE BLUE HERON, SOUTH FLORIDA. This slender, medium-sized heron flocks and nests with other wading birds throughout south Florida. Young little blues are white; the patchy plumage of maturing birds makes the species unique among herons.

FLORIDA BAY. No part of the state is more than 60 miles from salt water or rises more than 345 feet above sea level. Two million years ago, most of Florida lay under the ocean.

(Right) OVERSEAS HIGHWAY, FLORIDA KEYS. Stretching some 100 miles from Miami to Key West is the Overseas Highway. It was built on the roadbed of developer Henry Flagler's Florida East Coast Railroad Extension after tracks were destroyed by the Labor Day hurricane of 1935.

GREEN-BACKED HERON, SOUTH FLORIDA. The green-backed heron usually feeds and nests alone; when alarmed, it raises a shaggy black crest.

83

(Above and facing) CONCH HOUSES, KEY WEST. Combining elements of New England, Bahamian, Creole, and Victorian architecture, ships' carpenters built Key West's distinctive conch houses in the 19th century. Shutters, verandas, and the ornamental work known as gingerbread are characteristic of these wooden structures.

FORT JEFFERSON NATIONAL MONUMENT, DRY TORTUGAS. Construction on Fort Jefferson began in 1846. After the Civil War, the fort served as a prison. Samuel Mudd was jailed here for setting the broken leg of Abraham Lincoln's assassin John Wilkes Booth. Mudd's help during a yellow fever epidemic earned the doctor an early pardon.

BROWN PELICANS, SOUTH FLORIDA

Photography Credits

Matt Bradley: cover, pages 1, 20, 20-21, 28-29, 50, 51, 80-81, 84, 88, 89, 90-91, 91, and 92-93.

C.C. Lockwood: pages 2-3, 19, 38-39, 39, 40-41, and 94.

Florida Department of Commerce/Division of Tourism: pages 4-5, 46-47 (Glenn L. Hastings), 30-31 (Ralph L. Fortune), and 70 (Robert M. Overton).

Baron Wolman: pages 6-7, 48-49, 49, 55, 64, 70-71, 75, and 86.

Doug Morrison: page 8.

Ray Stanyard: pages 10, 14, 15, 16-17, 18-19, and 43.

The Walt Disney Company: page 12.

Doug Brown: page 13.

Ed Weigel: page 16.

Earl Henderson: pages 22, 22-23, and 26-27.

Buckeye Cellulose Corporation: page 24 (N.E. Thomas).

Tim Thompson: pages 25 and 76-77.

Nathan Benn: pages 29, 32, 32-33, 34, 34-35, 65, 72-73, 74-75, 77, 85, and 87.

Bernice Weiss: pages 30 and 47.

Red Morgan: pages 36 and 54.

National Aeronautics and Space Administration: page 37.

Kevin Fleming: pages 42 and 44-45.

Tony Arruza: pages 52-53.

Connie Toops: pages 56 and 82.

Bates Littlehales: pages 57, 60, 79, and 83.

Yogi Kaufman: pages 58, 59, 61, and 78.

Alto Adams, Jr.: pages 62-63.

Apa Photo Agency: page 63.

Robert Llewellyn: pages 66 and 67.

David J. Kaminsky: pages 68 and 69.

Talmadge E. Lewis: page 80.

Special thanks to AT&T whose generous gift of books to the state of Florida helped make this publication possible, and to Dixie Lee Nims and Lee H. Warner for their invaluable assistance.

SEAWEED, FLORIDA KEYS. Windrows festoon the sand after a
storm. During the hurricane season from June through November,
official warnings are issued when winds reach velocities of over
74 miles per hour.

(Left) SOMBRERO REEF, NEAR KNIGHTS KEY. Boats are essential to divers south of Biscayne Bay; the shallow coral reef system fringing the Florida Keys lies seaward from four to six miles. In summer, dives offer spectacular lateral visibility ranging from 60 to 100 feet.

CORAL REEF, FLORIDA KEYS. Coral reefs provide a habitat for numerous plants and fish and act as natural breakwaters for adjacent coastlines. Formed from the limestone skeletons of sedentary, colonial animals called polyps, they grow slowly, at an estimated rate of no more than 16 feet every 1,000 years.

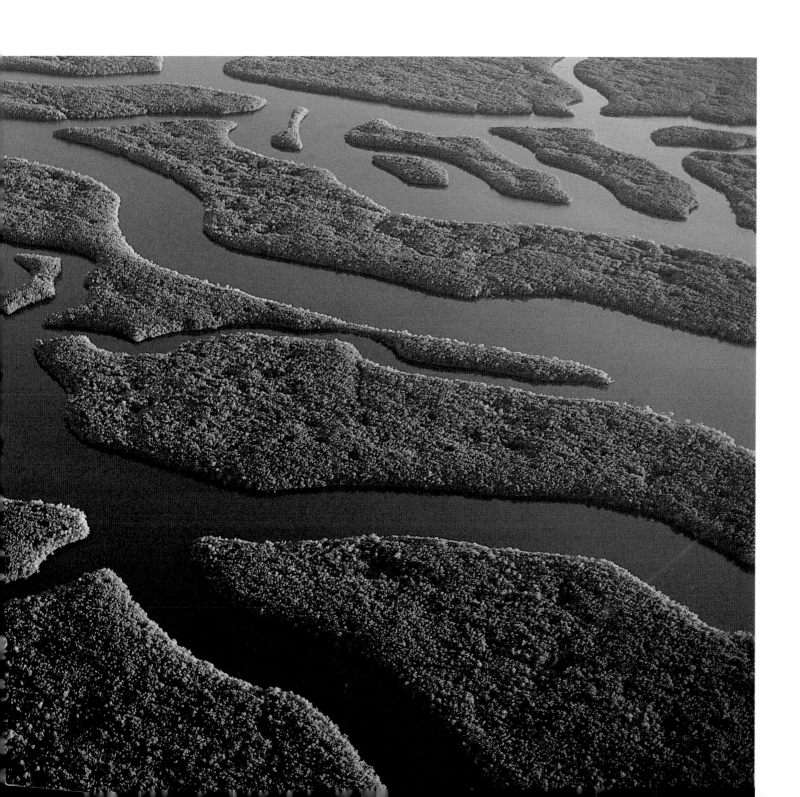

LOBSTER TRAPS, FLORIDA KEYS. The commercially harvested spiny lobster, also called the Florida crawfish, though lacking the Maine variety's meaty claws, is considered by many to be more flavorful.

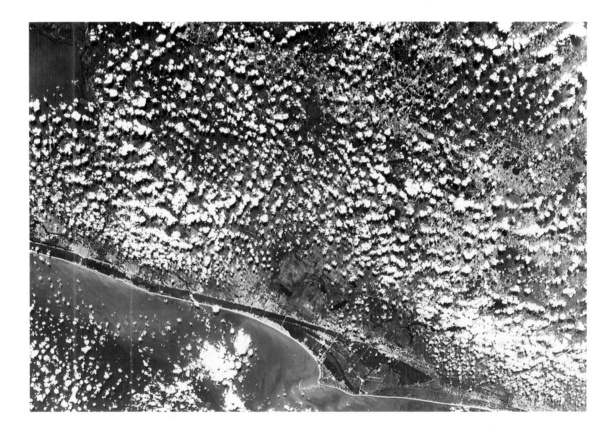

(Left) SHUTTLE LAUNCH, JOHN F. KENNEDY SPACE CENTER. The United States' first satellite was launched from Cape Canaveral in 1958; eleven years later the National Aeronautics and Space Administration put men on the moon.

AERIAL VIEW, FLORIDA'S EAST COAST. Manned space exploration is only a part of NASA's mission. Since the nation's first weather satellite was put into orbit in 1960, satellite observations have, for example, offered better understanding of ocean currents. This image was taken 124 nautical miles above the Kennedy Space Center by NASA's Large Format Camera.